# The Baroque Trumpet

*16 repertoire pieces from the Golden Age for trumpet in D
(or standard B♭ or piccolo) and keyboard*

*16 Repertoirestücke aus der Blütezeit des Barock für Trompete in D
(oder in B oder in Hoch-B) und Klavier*

*16 pièces de répertoire pour trompette en ré (ou trompette en si bémol
ou trompette piccolo) et clavier empruntées à l'âge d'or de la musique*

## Selected and arranged by John Miller

© 1997 by Faber Music Ltd
First published in 1997 by Faber Music Ltd
3 Queen Square London WC1N 3AU
Cover design by S & M Tucker
Music engraved by Stephen Keeley
Printed in England by Caligraving Ltd
All rights reserved
ISBN 0-571-51704-8

**FABER *ff* MUSIC**

# Foreword

This small collection has two aims: to introduce the player to the rich seam of trumpet repertoire of the Renaissance and Baroque periods, and to introduce pieces in such a manner that the skills of playing D trumpet and piccolo trumpet can be acquired *gradually*, building up range, stamina and finesse throughout the book. The level of difficulty is approximately from intermediate to advanced and beyond.

## The music

The pieces are all presented in modern performing editions. The keyboard accompaniments are, for the most part, realised from the original figured bass; in some cases, existing accompaniments have been simplified. Organ or harpsichord, if available, can be used, but piano will in all cases be effective. To achieve a smooth progression of challenge through the book, a few pieces have been transposed from original keys. Suggested indications of tempo, style, dynamics and phrasing have been added sparingly.

The Banchieri *Canzona* was not actually written for trumpet, but is taken from a set of five written for cornetto. On the other hand, Fantini's *Sonata detta del Niccolini* is from *Modo per imparare a sonare di tromba* of 1638 – and the Viviani pieces from one of the few baroque sources specifically composed for organ (or harpsichord) and trumpet, dated 1678. French music is represented by Delalande and Charpentier, both of whom wrote for the band of the Sun King at Versailles. The familiar Clarke *Rondeau* is from a *Suite de Clairque* contained in part books in the British Museum.

The German baroque repertoire includes an Air by Telemann, from *Getreuen Musikmeister* of 1728, and a transcription of Bach's chorale *Jesu Joy of Man's Desiring*. The collection ends with a transcription of a fine organ voluntary not composed for trumpet, but written in the "trumpet style" (for trumpet stop) by John Stanley.

## Technical notes

The collection has been purposely devised in two halves. The first is designed for either D trumpet, or alternatively standard B flat trumpet. However, the pieces in C major (concert pitch) may be performed on the E flat trumpet or soprano cornet – by transposing the D part down a semitone to A major, or, alternatively, on the C trumpet.

The second half of the collection introduces the piccolo trumpet as an alternative to the D trumpet. The piccolo trumpet is introduced later than the D trumpet, for its execution demands a really well-trained embouchure. The best piccolo trumpet set-up for pieces in D major (concert pitch) is in A, because of the resulting facile fingerings of played F major. The "piccolo A" is simply the normal B flat piccolo instrument, either with the tuning shank pulled out a semitone, or with a special shank (or tuning slide) inserted. Note that the other smaller slides MUST be pulled out proportionally, if the instrument is to be in tune. First tune the played middle G (sounding E at the top of the treble clef) with the piano. Then tune the played F one tone lower (sounding D). This will necessitate the first slide being drawn one or two mm. The third slide will then have to be drawn proportionally further – tune the played D (sounding B). If the instrument has a fourth valve, the fourth slide should be drawn around a centimetre, until you can play a sound octave F; from the played F on the first space of the treble clef to the F an octave lower (using first and fourth valves). Selection of a suitable mouthpiece, a well-developed embouchure, really firm support, and correct tongue position will all influence intonation and execution in the high register. *Progressive Studies for Trumpet*, by the editor of this collection, explains how these principles can be developed.

John Miller 1997

---

John Miller is one of Britain's leading brass teachers. He read music at King's College, Cambridge, and subsequently studied trumpet in the USA. He freelanced extensively in London, notably with the London Sinfonietta and the Philip Jones Brass Ensemble, and was a member of the Philharmonia Orchestra between 1977 and 1994. He is a founder member of the Wallace Collection.

He has been a professor of trumpet at the Guildhall School of Music and Drama, London, since 1979, a brass tutor of the National Youth Orchestra of Great Britain since 1991, and in 1993 was awarded an Honorary Fellowship of the Guildhall School. His teaching activities to date have included workshops in Australia, China, Finland, Germany, Japan, Spain, USA and the Paris Conservatoire.

# Vorwort

Diese kleine Sammlung möchte zweierlei erreichen: Zum einen soll dem Spieler ermöglicht werden, das umfangreiche Repertoire aus Renaissance und Barock kennenzulernen. Zum anderen aber sind die Stücke so angeordnet, daß Tonumfang, Ausdauer und musikalische Anforderung insgesamt zunehmen, das Spielen auf der Trompete in D und auf der Trompete in Hoch-B also zunehmend geläufiger wird.

## Zur den Werken

Alle Stücke werden in der heute üblichen Notationsweise vorgestellt. Die Klavierbegleitungen sind in den meisten Fällen aus den originalen Baßbezifferungen abgeleitet. In einigen Fällen wurden vorhandene Begleitungen vereinfacht. Die Stücke können nicht nur auf dem Klavier – dies ergibt auf jeden Fall befriedigende klangliche Resultate –, sondern wahlweise auch mit Orgel oder Cembalo begleitet werden. Einige Stücke wurden gegenüber der originalen Tonart transponiert, um bei der Abfolge der Stücke keine Sprünge hinsichtlich des Schwierigkeitsgrades zu bewirken. Der Herausgeber ergänzte einige wenige Hinweise zu Tempo, Stil, Dynamik und Phrasierung.

Banchieris *Canzona* ist im Original kein Werk für Trompete, sondern stammt aus einer Sammlung mit fünf Kanzonen für Zink. Fantinis *Sonata detta del Niccolini* dagegen stammt aus der Veröffentlichung *Modo per imparare a sonare di tromba* aus dem Jahr 1638, und die Stücke von Viviani aus einer 1678 datierten Quelle – übrigens eine der wenigen Quellen im Barock, die ausdrücklich für Orgel (oder Cembalo) und Trompete geschrieben sind. Die französische Musik wird durch Delalande und Charpentier repräsentiert, die beide für die Kapelle des Sonnenkönigs in Versailles komponierten. Das bekannte *Rondeau* von Clarke stammt aus einer *Suite de Clairque,* die in Stimmbüchern im British Museum überliefert ist.

Das Repertoire deutscher Barockmusik für Trompete umfaßt eine Air aus Telemanns 1728 publizierter Sammlung *Der Getreue Musikmeister* sowie eine Transkription von Bachs Choral "Jesus bleibet meine Freude", dem Schlußchoral aus der Kantate BWV 147 "Herz und Mund und Tat und Leben". Das Schlußstück der Sammlung bildet die Übertragung eines "im Stil einer Trompete" geschriebenen Orgelstückes von John Stanley, das im Original die entsprechende Registrierung auf der Orgel verlangt.

## Technische Hinweise

Die Ausgabe wurde ganz bewußt zweigeteilt. Der erste Teil ist für Trompete in D oder die übliche Trompete in B gedacht. Die Stücke in C-Dur (klingend) können jedoch auch auf der Trompete in Es oder auf dem Soprankornett ausgeführt werden, indem der Part für die Trompete in D um einen Halbton nach unten (A-Dur) transponiert wird. Auch die Ausführung auf der Trompete in C ist möglich.

Im zweiten Teil der Ausgabe wird die Hoch-B-Trompete als Alternative zur Trompete in D eingeführt. Dieses Instrument wird erst *nach* der Trompete in D vorgestellt, da sein Spiel eines gut trainierten Ansatzes bedarf. Für die Ausführung auf der Hoch-B-Trompete bietet sich eine Konstellation in A-Dur an (klingend D), da sich so die leichten Fingersätze wie bei F-Dur ergeben. Bei der Piccolo A-Trompete handelt es sich um das normale Instrument in Hoch-B, bei dem entweder der Zug für die Gesamtstimmung einen Halbton herausgezogen ist oder bei der ein spezieller A-Stift ergänzt wird. Die anderen Züge müssen entsprechend herausgezogen werden, um eine saubere Stimmung zu erreichen. Zuerst stimme man mit dem Klavier das $g'$ (klingend $e''$). Dann wird das $f'$ gestimmt (klingend $d''$). Hierbei wird man den Zug des ersten Ventils um einen oder zwei Millimeter herausziehen müssen. Der Zug des dritten Ventils muß dann entsprechend justiert werden, um den Ton $d$ zu spielen (klingend $h'$). Falls das Instrument ein viertes Ventil hat, sollte der vierte Zug um etwa einen Zentimeter herausgezogen werden, bis man eine saubere Oktave auf $f$ spielen kann (notiert $f'$ – $f$ unter Verwendung des ersten und vierten Ventils). Das sorgfältige Auswählen eines passenden Mundstückes, ein guter Ansatz, eine gute Stütze und die richtige Position der Zunge tragen zu korrekter Intonation und guter Ausführung im hohen Register bei. Der Autor der vorliegenden Sammlung erläutert in seinem Werk *Progressive Studies for Trumpet*, wie man diese ver- schiedenen Parameter entwickelt.

John Miller 1997

---

John Miller gehört zu Großbritanniens führenden Lehrern für Blechblasinstrumente. Er studierte am Kings College in Cambridge Musik und setzte dann seine musikalische Ausbildung mit einem Trompetenstudium in den USA fort. Er spielte in zahlreichen Ensembles in London, vor allem mit der London Sinfonietta und dem Philip Jones Brass Ensemble und war von 1977 bis 1994 Mitglied der Londoner Philharmoniker. Er ist Gründungsmitglied der Wallace Sammlung.

Von 1979 an war er Professor für Trompete an der Guildhall School of Music and Drama in London, seit 1991 unterrichtet er die Blechbläser des Englischen Jugendorchesters und 1993 wurde er Honorary Fellow an der Guildhall School. Im Laufe seiner vielseitigen Unterrichtspraxis hat er Meisterkurse in Australien, China, Finnland, Deutschland, Japan, Spanien, in den USA und am Pariser Konservatorium abgehalten.

# Canzona 5

Adriano Banchieri
(1567-1634)

5

6

## Sonata detta del Niccolini

Girolamo Fantini
(c.1600 fl. 1630-38)

# Air

Georg Philipp Telemann
(1681-1767)

# Jesu, Joy of Man's Desiring

Johann Sebastian Bach (1685-1750)
arr. Leslie Pearson

12

## Air en Echo

Michel-Richard Delalande
(1657-1726)

# Four Pieces from Sonata Prima
## (1678)

*i*

Giovanni Bonaventura Viviani
(1638-c.1692)

Maestoso ♩ = 84

18

ii

*iii*

*iv*

# Come Ye Sons of Art

Henry Purcell
(1659-95)

**D.C. poi al Coda**

**CODA**

# Minuet

Jeremiah Clarke
(c.1674-1707)

**Andante** ♩ = 132

*trumpet tacet on repeat*

*trumpet 2nd time ad lib.*

\* Trumpet either *tacet* 2nd time or play with embellishments.
  Trompete: bei der Wiederholung *tacet* oder Ausführung mit verzierungen.

# Ecossaise

Jeremiah Clarke

# Rondeau

Jeremiah Clarke

26

*trumpet play 2nd time only*

# Rondeau from Te Deum

Marc-Antoine Charpentier
(1645-50-1704)

In this piece and in much French baroque music, try playing the quavers *inégales*: ♫ becomes ♩³♪ with the second note 'lifted'.

In diesem Stück sollte man – wie vielfach in französischer Barockmusik – die Achtelnoten als *notes inégales* spielen: aus ♫ wird ♩³♪, wobei die zweite Note leichter gespielt wird.

# Trumpet Tune

Henry Purcell
(1659-95)

## Voluntary

John Stanley
(1713-86)

32

Orson Owl,
*page 18*

CW00329460

# Table of Contents

Bernard Buzzard,
*page 23*

# Pierre Parrot

## Skill Level

 EASY

## Finished Measurement

9½ inches tall

## Materials

- Premier Yarns Deborah Norville Everyday Soft Worsted medium (worsted) weight acrylic yarn (4 oz/203 yds/113g per skein):
  1 skein each #1038 electric green, #1028 mustard and #1022 bittersweet
  2 yds each #1012 black and #1001 snow white
- Size G/6/4mm crochet hook or size needed to obtain gauge
- Tapestry needle
- Polyester fiberfill
- 12-inch green chenille stems: 2
- Stitch marker
- Small hairbrush

## Gauge

4 sc = 1 inch; 4 sc rows = 1 inch

## Pattern Notes

Weave in ends as work progresses.

Work in continuous rounds; do not join or turn unless otherwise stated.

Mark first stitch of round. Move marker up with each round.

Join with slip stitch as indicated unless otherwise stated.

## Parrot

### Head & Body

**Rnd 1:** With green and starting at top of Head, ch 2, 8 sc in 2nd ch from hook, **do not join, place marker** (see Pattern Notes). (8 sc)

**Rnd 2:** 2 sc in each sc around. (16 sc)

**Rnd 3:** [Sc in next sc, 2 sc in next sc] around. (24 sc)

**Rnd 4:** Sc in each sc around.

**Rnd 5:** [Sc in each of next 2 sc, 2 sc in next sc] around. (32 sc)

**Rnds 6 & 7:** Rep rnd 4.

**Rnd 8:** [Sc in each of next 3 sc, 2 sc in next sc] around. (40 sc)

**Rnd 9:** Sc in each sc around, **join** (see Pattern Notes) in first sc. Fasten off.

**Rnd 10:** Join mustard with sc in first sc of last rnd, sc in each rem sc around.

**Rnds 11–19:** Rep rnd 4.

**Rnd 20:** [Sc in each of next 3 sc, **sc dec** (see Stitch Guide) in next 2 sc] around. (32 sc)

**Rnd 21:** Rep rnd 4.

**Rnd 22:** [Sc in each of next 3 sc, sc dec in next 2 sc] 6 times, sc in each of next 2 sc, join in first sc. Fasten off. (26 sc)

**Rnd 23:** Join green with sc in first sc of last rnd, sc in each rem sc around.

Stuff with fiberfill.

**Rnd 24:** [Sc in each of next 3 sc, 2 sc in next sc] 6 times, sc in each of next 2 sc. (32 sc)

**Rnd 25:** [Sc in each of next 3 sc, 2 sc in next sc] around. *(40 sc)*

**Rnds 26 & 27:** Rep rnd 4.

**Rnd 28:** [Sc in each of next 4 sc, 2 sc in next sc] around. *(48 sc)*

**Rnds 29 & 30:** Rep rnd 4.

**Rnd 31:** [Sc in each of next 5 sc, 2 sc in next sc] around. *(56 sc)*

**Rnds 32–37:** Rep rnd 4.

**Rnd 38:** [Sc in each of next 5 sc, sc dec in next 2 sc] around. *(48 sc)*

**Rnds 39 & 40:** Rep rnd 4.

Stuff.

**Rnd 41:** [Sc in each of next 4 sc, sc dec in next 2 sc] around. *(40 sc)*

**Rnd 42:** Rep rnd 4.

**Rnd 43:** [Sc in each of next 3 sc, sc dec in next 2 sc] around. *(32 sc)*

**Rnd 44:** [Sc in each of next 2 sc, sc dec in next 2 sc] around. *(24 sc)*

**Rnd 45:** [Sc in next sc, sc dec in next 2 sc] around. *(16 sc)*

Stuff.

**Rnd 46:** [Sc dec in next 2 sc] around. *(8 sc)*

**Rnds 47 & 48:** Rep rnd 46. At end of last rnd, leaving 6-inch end for sewing, fasten off. *(2 sc)*

Sew opening closed.

## Beak

**Rnd 1:** With bittersweet, ch 20, join in first ch to form ring, sc in each ch around. *(20 sc)*

**Rnd 2:** Sc in each sc around.

**Rnds 3–11:** Rep rnd 2.

**Rnd 12:** [Sc dec in next 2 sc] around. *(10 sc)*

**Rnds 13 & 14:** Rep rnd 2.

**Rnd 15:** Rep rnd 12. *(5 sc)*

**Rnd 16:** [Sc dec in next 2 sc] twice, sc in next sc. Leaving 6-inch end for sewing, fasten off. *(3 sc)*

Sew opening closed. Stuff Beak, leaving rnds 15 and 16 unstuffed. Sew rnd 1 to Head between rnds 9–19. Referring to photo for placement and with black, **backstitch** *(see illustration)* mouth lines on sides of Beak.

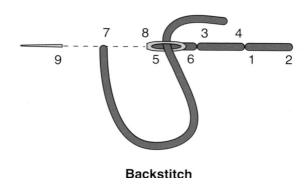

**Backstitch**

## Eye
**Make 2.**

With white, ch 4, 2 sc in 2nd ch from hook, sc in next ch, 2 sc in last ch, working in unused lps on opposite side of foundation ch, sc in next ch, join in first sc. Fasten off. *(6 sc)*

## Pupil
**Make 2.**

With green, ch 2, 4 sc in 2nd ch from hook, join in first sc. Fasten off.

Sew over 1 end of each Eye. Sew Eyes to Head on each side of Beak.

## Eyelid
**Make 2.**

**Row 1:** With mustard, ch 2, 3 sc in 2nd ch from hook, turn. *(3 sc)*

**Row 2:** Ch 1, 2 sc in first sc, sc in next sc, 2 sc in last sc, turn. *(5 sc)*

**Row 3:** Ch 1, sc in each of first 2 sc, 2 sc in next sc, sc in each of last 2 sc. Fasten off. *(6 sc)*

Sew over top half of each Eye.

## Foot
**Make 2.**

**Rnd 1:** With bittersweet, ch 12, join in first ch to form ring, sc in each ch around. *(12 sc)*

**Rnd 2:** Sc in each sc around.

**Rnds 3–9:** Rep rnd 2.

### First Toe
**Rnd 10:** Sc in each of next 3 sc, sk next 6 sc, sc in each of next 3 sc. *(6 sc)*

**Rnd 11:** Rep rnd 2.

**Rnd 12:** [Sc dec in next 2 sc] 3 times. *(3 sc)*

**Rnd 13:** Sc dec in next 2 sc, sc in next sc. Leaving 5-inch end for sewing, fasten off. *(2 sc)*

Sew opening closed.

### 2nd Toe
**Rnd 1:** Join bittersweet with sc in 4th sc on rnd 9, sc in each of next 5 sc. *(6 sc)*

**Rnds 2–4:** Rep rnds 11–13 of First Toe.

Stuff.

Flatten rnd 1, sew opening at top of Foot closed. Sew Feet to rnds 44 and 45 at bottom front of Body. Tack to rnd 42 of Body to help balance.

## Wing
**Make 2.**

**Rnd 1:** With green, ch 2, 6 sc in 2nd ch from hook. *(6 sc)*

**Rnd 2:** 2 sc in each sc around. *(12 sc)*

**Rnd 3:** [Sc in next sc, 2 sc in next sc] around. *(18 sc)*

**Rnd 4:** [Sc in each of next 2 sc, 2 sc in next sc] around. *(24 sc)*

**Rnd 5:** [Sc in each of next 3 sc, 2 sc in next sc] around. *(30 sc)*

**Rnd 6:** Sc in each sc around.

**Rnd 7:** [Sc in each of next 4 sc, 2 sc in next sc] around. *(36 sc)*

**Rnd 8:** [Sc in each of next 5 sc, 2 sc in next sc] around, join in first sc. Do not fasten off. *(42 sc)*

Fold piece in half. Working through both thicknesses, sc in each st across. Fasten off. *(21 sc)*

## Fringe
For Fringe, cut 1 strand of green 4½ inches long. Fold strand in half, insert hook in st, pull folded end through, pull ends through fold, pull ends to tighten knot. Fray ends of yarn and brush to fluff. Work fringe in each st of row 9 across bottom edge of Wing. Curving top edge of Wings and referring to photo for placement, sew to sides of Body over rnds 25–35.

## Tail Feather
**Make 3.**

With green, ch 12, sc in 2nd ch from hook, sc in each of next 9 chs, 3 sc in next ch, working in unused lps on opposite side of foundation ch, sc in each of next 10 chs. Fasten off. *(23 sc)*

Work Fringe in each st around edge of Feather same as for Wing.

Cut piece of chenille stem 4½ inches long. Sew along center back of each Feather, covering seam completely. Place 1 end of all 3 Feathers tog. Sew to back of Body 3½ inches from neck.

For top knots, work Fringe in each sc of rnd 1 at top of Head. ●

# Ophelia Ostrich

## Skill Level

 EASY

## Finished Measurement

21 inches tall

## Materials

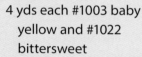

- Premier Yarns Deborah Norville Everyday Soft Worsted medium (worsted) weight acrylic yarn (4 oz/203 yds/ 113g per skein):
    2 skeins each #1001 snow white and #1012 black
    4 yds each #1003 baby yellow and #1022 bittersweet
- Size G/6/4mm crochet hook or size needed to obtain gauge
- Tapestry needle
- 4-inch x 6-inch piece of plastic canvas
- Polyester fiberfill
- Stitch marker

## Gauge

4 sc = 1 inch; 4 sc rows = 1 inch

## Pattern Notes

Weave in ends as work progresses.

Work in continuous rounds; do not join or turn unless otherwise stated.

Mark first stitch of round. Move marker up with each round.

Join with slip stitch as indicated unless otherwise stated.

## Special Stitch

**Loop stitch (lp st):** Insert hook in indicated st, wrap yarn clockwise twice around finger, insert hook from left to right through all lps on finger, pull lps on hook through st, drop lps from finger, yo, pull through all 4 lps on hook.

## Ostrich

### Head & Neck

**Rnd 1:** Starting at top of Head with white, ch 2, 6 sc in 2nd ch from hook, **do not join, place marker** *(see Pattern Notes). (6 sc)*

**Rnd 2:** 2 **lp sts** *(see Special Stitch)* in each sc around. *(12 lp sts)*

**Rnd 3:** [Sc in next st, 2 sc in next st] around. *(18 sc)*

**Rnd 4:** [Lp st in each of next 2 sc, 2 lp sts in next sc] around. *(24 lp sts)*

**Rnd 5:** [Sc in each of next 3 sts, 2 sc in next st] around. *(30 sc)*

**Rnd 6:** [Lp st in each of next 4 sc, 2 lp sts in next sc] around. *(36 lp sts)*

**Rnd 7:** Sc in each st around.

**Rnd 8:** [Lp st in each of next 5 sc, 2 lp sts in next sc] around. *(42 lp sts)*

**Rnd 9:** Rep rnd 7.

**Rnd 10:** Lp st in each sc around.

**Rnds 11–14:** [Rep rnds 9 and 10 alternately] twice.

**Rnd 15:** [Sc in each of next 5 sts, **sc dec** *(see Stitch Guide)* in next 2 sts] around. *(36 sc)*

**Rnd 16:** Rep rnd 10.

**Rnd 17:** [Sc in next st, sc dec in next 2 sts] around. *(24 sc)*

**Rnd 18:** Lp st in each sc around, join in first sc, turn.

Turn lps to outside.

Stuff with fiberfill.

**Rnd 19:** [Sc in next st, sc dec in next 2 sts] around. *(16 sc)*

**Rnds 20–48:** Rep rnd 7. At end of last rnd, **join** *(see Pattern Notes)* in first sc. Fasten off.

Sew 6-inch edges of plastic canvas tog to form tube. Stuff tube and upper 2 inches of Neck. Insert tube into Neck, leaving 1 inch of tube exposed.

## Body

**Rnd 1:** Starting at back with white, ch 2, 4 sc in 2nd ch from hook. *(4 sc)*

**Rnd 2:** 2 lp sts in each sc around. *(8 lp sts)*

**Rnd 3:** [Sc in next st, 2 sc in next st] around. *(12 sc)*

**Rnd 4:** [Lp st in each of next 3 sc, 2 lp sts in next sc] around. *(15 lp sts)*

**Rnd 5:** Sc in each st around.

**Rnd 6:** [Lp st in each of next 4 sc, 2 lp sts in next sc] around. *(18 lp sts)*

**Rnd 7:** Rep rnd 5.

**Rnd 8:** [Lp st in each of next 2 sc, 2 lp sts in next sc] around. *(24 lp sts)*

**Rnd 9:** Rep rnd 5.

**Rnd 10:** [Lp st in each of next 3 sc, 2 lp sts in next sc] around. *(30 lp sts)*

**Rnd 11:** Rep rnd 5.

**Rnd 12:** [Lp st in each of next 4 sc, 2 lp sts in next sc] around. *(36 lp sts)*

**Rnd 13:** Sc in each st around, join in first sc. Fasten off.

**Rnd 14:** Join black in first sc, [lp st in each of next 5 sc, 2 lp sts in next sc] around. *(42 lp sts)*

**Rnd 15:** Rep rnd 5.

**Rnd 16:** [Lp st in each of next 6 sc, 2 lp sts in next sc] around. *(48 lp sts)*

**Rnd 17:** Rep rnd 5.

**Rnd 18:** Lp st in each st around.

**Rnds 19–28:** [Rep rnds 17 and 18 alternately] 5 times.

**Rnd 29:** Rep rnd 17.

**Row 30:** Now working in rows, sl st in each of next 3 sc, lp st in each of next 44 sc, leaving last sc unworked, turn. *(44 lp sts)*

**Row 31:** Ch 1, sc in each of first 2 sts, [sc dec in next 2 sts, sc in each of next 3 sts] 8 times, sc in next st, leaving last st unworked, turn. *(35 sc)*

**Row 32:** Ch 1, lp st in each sc across, turn.

**Rnd 33:** Now working in rnds, ch 1, sc in same st as beg ch-1, sc dec in next 2 sts, [sc in next st, sc dec in next 2 sts] 10 times, sc in each of next 2 sts, ch 4, join in first sc, turn. *(24 sts, 4 chs)*

**Rnd 34:** Ch 1, lp st in each of next 4 chs, lp st in each of next 24 sts. *(28 lp sts)*

**Rnd 35:** *Sc in next st, [sc dec in next 2 sts] 4 times, rep from * twice, sc in last st. *(16 sc)*

**Rnd 36:** Lp st in each st around.

Turn lps to outside and stuff tightly.

**Rnd 37:** [Sc dec in next 2 sts] 8 times. *(8 sc)*

**Rnd 38:** [Sc dec in next 2 sc] 4 times. Fasten off. *(4 sc)*

Sew opening closed. Insert 1-inch plastic canvas of Neck into opening on Body. Sew last row of Neck to Body opening.

## Beak

**Rnd 1:** With bittersweet, ch 2, 4 sc in 2nd ch from hook. *(4 sc)*

**Rnd 2:** 2 sc in each sc around. *(8 sc)*

**Rnd 3:** Sc in each sc around.

**Rnd 4:** [Sc in each of next 3 sc, 2 sc in next sc] around. *(10 sc)*

**Rnds 5–7:** Rep rnd 3.

**Rnd 8:** Sc in each sc around, join in first sc. Fasten off.

Stuff and sew to front of Head over rnds 13 and 14. With tapestry needle and black, embroider **French knots** *(see illustration)* on top of Beak for nostrils.

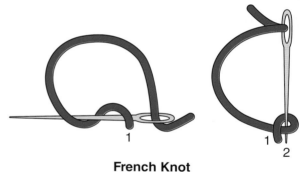

**French Knot**

## Eye
**Make 2.**

With black, ch 2, 8 sc in 2nd ch from hook, join in first sc. Fasten off. Sew to front of head above Beak 2¼ inches apart.

## Eyelid
**Make 2.**

**Row 1:** With yellow, ch 2, 5 sc in 2nd ch from hook, turn. *(5 sc)*

**Row 2:** Ch 1, sc in each sc across. Fasten off.

Sew over top half of each Eye.

## Leg
**Make 2.**

**Rnd 1:** With black, ch 30, join in first ch to form ring, ch 1, sc in each ch around. *(30 sc)*

**Rnd 2:** Lp st in each sc around.

**Rnd 3:** Sc in each st around.

**Rnds 4–7:** [Rep rnds 2 and 3 alternately] twice.

**Rnd 8:** Rep rnd 2.

**Rnd 9:** [Sc in each of next 3 sts, sc dec in next 2 sts] around. *(24 sc)*

**Rnd 10:** Rep rnd 2.

**Rnd 11:** [Sc in each of next 2 sts, sc dec in next 2 sts] around. *(18 sc)*

**Rnd 12:** Lp st in each sc around, join in first st. Fasten off. Turn lps to outside.

**Rnd 13:** Join white with sc in any st of last rnd, sc in each rem st around.

**Rnd 14:** Rep rnd 3.

**Rnd 15:** [Sc in each of next 2 sc, sc dec in next 2 sc] 4 times, sc in each of next 2 sc. *(14 sc)*

**Rnds 16 & 17:** Rep rnd 14.

**Rnd 18:** [Sc in each of next 5 sc, sc dec in next 2 sc] around. *(12 sc)*

**Rnds 19–30:** Rep rnd 3.

**Rnd 31:** Sc in each sc around, join in first sc. Fasten off.

## Foot
**Make 2.**

**Rnd 1:** With bittersweet, ch 2, 6 sc in 2nd ch from hook. *(6 sc)*

**Rnd 2:** 2 sc in each sc around. *(12 sc)*

**Rnd 3:** [Sc in each of next 3 sc, 2 sc in next sc] around. *(15 sc)*

**Rnd 4:** Sc in each sc around.

Stuff.

### First Toe
**Rnd 5:** Sc in each of next 5 sc, leave rem sc unworked. *(5 sc)*

**Rnd 6:** Sc in each sc around.

**Rnds 7–10:** Rep rnd 6.

**Rnd 11:** Sc in each sc around. Leaving 6-inch end for sewing, fasten off.

Stuff. Weave end through outer lp of each sc, pull tight and fasten off.

### 2nd Toe
**Rnd 1:** Join bittersweet with sc in 6th sc on rnd 4 of Foot, sc in each of next 2 sc, sk next 5 sc, sc in each of last 2 sc. *(5 sc)*

**Rnds 2–7:** Rep rnds 6–11 of First Toe.

### 3rd Toe
**Rnd 1:** Join bittersweet with sc in 9th sc on rnd 4 of Foot, sc in each of next 4 sc. *(5 sc)*

**Rnds 2–7:** Rep rnds 6–11 of First Toe.

Sew openings between Toes closed. Sew rnds 2–4 of Foot to last rnd of Leg. Stuff Legs and sew rnd 1 of each Leg to bottom of Body over rnds 14–27. Tack Legs tog 2 inches from Body. ●

# Percival Pelican

## Skill Level

 EASY

## Finished Measurement

13 inches tall

## Materials

- Premier Yarns Deborah Norville Everyday Soft Worsted medium (worsted) weight acrylic yarn (4 oz/203 yds/113g per skein):
    1 skein each #1001 snow white and #1022 bittersweet
    2 yds #1012 black
- Size G/6/4mm crochet hook or size needed to obtain gauge
- Tapestry needle
- Polyester fiberfill
- Stitch marker

*Need help?*
**StitchGuide.com**
ILLUSTRATED GUIDES
HOW-TO VIDEOS

## Gauge

4 sc = 1 inch; 4 sc rows = 1 inch

## Pattern Notes

Weave in ends as work progresses.

Work in continuous rounds; do not join or turn unless otherwise stated.

Mark first stitch of round. Move marker up with each round.

Join with slip stitch as indicated unless otherwise stated.

## Pelican

### Head & Beak

**Rnd 1:** Starting at top of Head with white, ch 2, 6 sc in 2nd ch from hook, **do not join, place marker** *(see Pattern Notes). (6 sc)*

**Rnd 2:** 2 sc in each sc around. *(12 sc)*

**Rnd 3:** [Sc in next sc, 2 sc in next sc] around. *(18 sc)*

**Rnd 4:** [Sc in each of next 2 sc, 2 sc in next st] around. *(24 sc)*

**Rnd 5:** Sc in each sc around.

**Rnd 6:** [Sc in each of next 3 sc, 2 sc in next st] around. *(30 sc)*

**Rnd 7:** [Sc in each of next 4 sc, 2 sc in next sc] around. *(36 sc)*

**Rnds 8–12:** Rep rnd 5.

**Rnd 13:** [Sc in each of next 4 sc, **sc dec** *(see Stitch Guide)* in next 2 sc] around. *(30 sc)*

**Rnd 14:** Rep rnd 5.

**Rnd 15:** [Sc in each of next 5 sc, sc dec in next 2 sc] 4 times, sc in each of next 2 sc, **join** *(see Pattern Notes)* in first sc. Fasten off. *(26 sc)*

Stuff with fiberfill.

**Rnd 16:** Join bittersweet with sc in first sc, sc in next sc, [2 sc in next sc, sc in each of next 3 sc] around. *(32 sc)*

**Rnd 17:** [Sc in each of next 7 sc, 2 sc in next sc] around. *(36 sc)*

**Rnd 18:** Rep rnd 5.

**Rnd 19:** [Sc in each of next 5 sc, 2 sc in next sc] around. *(42 sc)*

**Rnds 20–28:** Rep rnd 5.

**Rnd 29:** [Sc in each of next 8 sc, sc dec in next 2 sc] 4 times, sc in each of next 2 sc. *(38 sc)*

**Rnd 30:** [Sc dec in next 2 sc, sc in each of next 7 sc] 4 times, sc in each of next 2 sc. *(34 sc)*

**Rnd 31:** [Sc in each of next 6 sc, sc dec in next 2 sc] 4 times, sc in each of next 2 sc. *(30 sc)*

**Rnd 32:** [Sc dec in next 2 sc, sc in each of next 5 sc] 4 times, sc in each of next 2 sc. *(26 sc)*

**Rnd 33:** [Sc in each of next 4 sc, sc dec in next 2 sc] 4 times, sc in each of next 2 sc. *(22 sc)*

**Rnd 34:** [Sc dec in next 2 sc, sc in each of next 3 sc] 4 times, sc in each of next 2 sc. *(18 sc)*

**Rnd 35:** [Sc dec in next 2 sc] around. *(9 sc)*

Stuff.

**Rnd 36:** [Sc dec in next 2 sc] 4 times, sc in next sc, join in first sc. Leaving 5-inch end for sewing, fasten off. *(5 sc)*

Sew opening closed.

## Eye
**Make 2.**

**Rnd 1:** With white, ch 2, 6 sc in 2nd ch from hook. *(6 sc)*

**Rnd 2:** [3 sc in next sc, sc in each of next 2 sc] around. *(10 sc)*

**Rnd 3:** Sc in next sc, 3 sc in next sc, sc in each of next 4 sc, 3 sc in next sc, sc in each of next 3 sc. *(14 sc)*

**Rnd 4:** Sc in each sc around.

**Rnd 5:** [Sc in next sc, sc dec in next 2 sc] 4 times, sc in each of next 2 sc, join in first sc. Fasten off. *(10 sc)*

Stuff.

Sew to Head just above Beak. Referring to photo and with tapestry needle and black, **backstitch** *(see illustration)* across top of each Eye. With black, embroider **French knot** *(see illustration)* in center of each line for pupil. With black, embroider **straight stitches** *(see illustration)* for nostrils 1 inch apart at top of Beak and backstitches for mouth line around sides of Beak.

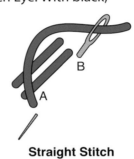

**Straight Stitch**

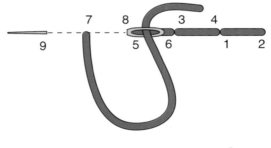

**Backstitch**

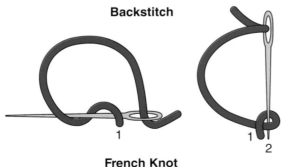

**French Knot**

## Body

**Rnd 1:** With white, ch 20, join in first ch to form ring, sc in each ch around. *(20 sc)*

**Rnd 2:** Sc in each sc around.

**Rnds 3–6:** Rep rnd 2.

**Rnd 7:** [Sc in each of next 3 sc, 2 sc in next sc] around. *(25 sc)*

**Rnd 8:** [Sc in each of next 4 sc, 2 sc in next sc] around. *(30 sc)*

**Rnd 9:** [Sc in each of next 5 sc, 2 sc in next sc] around. *(35 sc)*

**Rnd 10:** Rep rnd 2.

**Rnd 11:** [Sc in each of next 6 sc, 2 sc in next sc] around. *(40 sc)*

**Rnd 12:** [Sc in each of next 7 sc, 2 sc in next sc] around. *(45 sc)*

**Rnd 13:** [Sc in each of next 8 sc, 2 sc in next sc] around. *(50 sc)*

**Rnd 14:** Rep rnd 2.

**Rnd 15:** [Sc in each of next 9 sc, 2 sc in next sc] around. *(55 sts)*

**Rnd 16:** [Sc in each of next 10 sc, 2 sc in next sc] around. *(60 sc)*

**Rnd 17:** [Sc in each of next 11 sc, 2 sc in next sc] around. *(65 sc)*

**Rnds 18 & 19:** Rep rnd 2.

**Rnd 20:** [Sc in each of next 12 sc, 2 sc in next sc] around. *(70 sc)*

**Rnds 21–28:** Rep rnd 2.

**Rnd 29:** [Sc in each of next 9 sc, sc dec in next 2 sc] 6 times, sc in each of next 4 sc. *(64 sc)*

**Rnd 30:** [Sc in each of next 8 sc, sc dec in next 2 sc] 6 times, sc in each of next 4 sc. *(58 sc)*

**Rnd 31:** [Sc in each of next 7 sc, sc dec in next 2 sc] 6 times, sc in each of next 4 sc. *(52 sc)*

**Rnd 32:** [Sc in each of next 6 sc, sc dec in next 2 sc] 6 times, sc in each of next 4 sc. *(46 sc)*

**Rnd 33:** [Sc in each of next 5 sc, sc dec in next 2 sc] 6 times, sc in each of next 4 sc. *(40 sc)*

**Rnd 34:** [Sc in each of next 4 sc, sc dec in next 2 sc] 6 times, sc in each of next 4 sc. *(34 sc)*

**Rnd 35:** [Sc in each of next 3 sc, sc dec in next 2 sc] 6 times, sc in each of next 4 sc. *(28 sc)*

**Rnd 36:** [Sc in each of next 2 sc, sc dec in next 2 sc] 6 times, sc in each of next 4 sc. *(22 sc)*

**Rnd 37:** [Sc in next sc, sc dec in next 2 sc] 6 times, sc in each of next 4 sc. *(16 sc)*

Stuff.

**Rnd 38:** [Sc dec in next 2 sc] 8 times. *(8 sc)*

**Rnd 39:** [Sc dec in next 2 sc] 4 times. Leaving 6-inch end for sewing, fasten off. *(4 sc)*

Sew opening closed. Sew Head to rnd 1 of Body.

## Wing
**Make 2.**

**Rnds 1–4:** Rep rnds 1–4 of Head.

**Rnd 5:** [Sc in each of next 3 sc, 2 sc in next sc] around. *(30 sc)*

**Rnd 6:** [Sc in each of next 4 sc, 2 sc in next sc] around. *(36 sc)*

**Rnd 7:** [Sc in each of next 5 sc, 2 sc in next sc] around. *(42 sc)*

**Rnd 8:** [Sc in each of next 6 sc, 2 sc in next sc] around. *(48 sc)*

**Rnd 9:** [Sc in each of next 7 sc, 2 sc in next sc] around. *(54 sc)*

**Rnd 10:** [Sc in each of next 8 sc, 2 sc in next sc] around. *(60 sc)*

**Rnd 11:** [Sc in each of next 9 sc, 2 sc in next sc] around, join in first sc. Do not fasten off. *(66 sc)*

Fold piece in half; working through both thicknesses, sc in each st across. Fasten off. *(33 sc)*

Sew upper half of straight edge of Wings to sides of Body over rnds 9–17.

## Foot
**Make 2.**

**Rnd 1:** With bittersweet, ch 2, 6 sc in 2nd ch from hook. *(6 sc)*

**Rnd 2:** 2 sc in each sc around. *(12 sc)*

**Rnd 3:** Sc in each sc around.

**Rnds 4–18:** Rep rnd 3.

Stuff.

**Rnd 19:** [Sc in next sc, 2 sc in next sc] around. *(18 sc)*

### First Toe
**Rnd 20:** Sc in each of next 6 sc, leave rem sc unworked. *(6 sc)*

**Rnds 21–25:** Rep rnd 3.

Stuff.

**Rnd 26:** [Sc dec in next 2 sc] around until opening is closed. Fasten off.

### 2nd Toe
**Rnd 1:** Join bittersweet with sc in 7th sc on rnd 19, sc in each of next 5 sc, leave rem sc unworked. *(6 sc)*

**Rnds 2–7:** Rep rnds 21–25 of First Toe.

### 3rd Toe
**Rnd 1:** Join bittersweet with sc in 13th sc on rnd 19, sc in each of next 5 sc. *(6 sc)*

**Rnds 2–7:** Rep rnds 21–25 of First Toe.

Sew opening between Toes closed. Referring to photo for placement, sew Feet to bottom of Body. ●

# Tyrone Toucan

## Skill Level

 **EASY**

## Finished Measurement

10½ inches tall

## Materials

- Premier Yarns Deborah Norville Everyday Soft Worsted medium (worsted) weight acrylic yarn (4 oz/203 yds/113g per skein):
    2 skeins #1012 black
    1 skein each #1003 baby yellow, #1028 mustard and #1001 snow white
    3 yds #1017 azure
- Size H/8/5mm crochet hook or size needed to obtain gauge
- Tapestry needle
- Polyester fiberfill
- Stitch marker

## Gauge

7 sc = 2 inches; 7 sc rows = 2 inches

## Pattern Notes

Weave in ends as work progresses.

Work in continuous rounds; do not join or turn unless otherwise stated.

Mark first stitch of round. Move marker up with each round.

Join with slip stitch as indicated unless otherwise stated.

Chain-3 at beginning of row counts as first double crochet unless otherwise stated.

## Buzzard

### Head & Body

**Rnd 1:** With black and starting at top of Head, ch 2, 8 sc in 2nd ch from hook, **do not join, place marker** *(see Pattern Notes). (8 sc)*

**Rnd 2:** 2 sc in each sc around. *(16 sc)*

**Rnd 3:** [Sc in next sc, 2 sc in next sc] around. *(24 sc)*

**Rnd 4:** Sc in each sc around.

**Rnd 5:** Rep rnd 4.

**Rnd 6:** [Sc in each of next 2 sc, 2 sc in next sc] around. *(32 sc)*

**Rnd 7:** Rep rnd 4.

**Rnd 8:** [Sc in each of next 3 sc, 2 sc in next sc] around. *(40 sc)*

**Rnds 9–16:** Rep rnd 4.

**Rnd 17:** Rep rnd 8. *(50 sc)*

**Rnds 18 & 19:** Rep rnd 4.

**Rnd 20:** [Sc in each of next 4 sc, 2 sc in next sc] around. *(60 sc)*

**Rnds 21 & 22:** Rep rnd 4.

**Rnd 23:** [Sc in each of next 5 sc, 2 sc in next sc] around. *(70 sc)*

**Rnds 24–44:** Rep rnd 4.

**Rnd 45:** [Sc in each of next 5 sc, **sc dec** *(see Stitch Guide)* in next 2 sc] around. *(60 sc)*

**Rnd 46:** [Sc in each of next 4 sc, sc dec in next 2 sc] around. *(50 sc)*

**Rnd 47:** [Sc in each of next 3 sc, sc dec in next 2 sc] around. *(40 sc)*

**Rnd 48:** [Sc in each of next 2 sc, sc dec in next 2 sc] around. *(30 sc)*

**Rnd 49:** [Sc in next sc, sc dec in next 2 sc] around. *(20 sc)*

Stuff with fiberfill.

**Rnd 50:** [Sc dec in next 2 sc] 10 times. *(10 sc)*

**Rnd 51:** [Sc dec in next 2 sc] 5 times. Leaving 6-inch end for sewing, fasten off. *(5 sc)*

Sew opening closed.

## Beak
**Rnd 1:** With yellow, ch 30, **join** *(see Pattern Notes)* in first ch to form ring, sc in each ch around. *(30 sc)*

**Rnd 2:** Sc in each sc around.

**Rnds 3–15:** Rep rnd 2.

**Rnd 16:** [Sc dec in next 2 sc, sc in next sc] twice, sc in each rem sc around. *(28 sc)*

**Rnds 17 & 18:** Rep rnd 2.

**Rnds 19–33:** [Rep rnds 16–18 consecutively] 5 times. *(18 sc at end of last rnd)*

**Rnd 34:** [Sc dec in next 2 sc, sc in next sc] 3 times, sc in each rem sc around. *(15 sc)*

**Rnd 35:** Rep rnd 2.

**Rnd 36:** Rep rnd 34. *(12 sc)*

**Rnds 37–39:** Rep rnd 16. *(6 sc at end of last rnd)*

**Rnd 40:** [Sc dec in next 2 sc] 3 times. Leaving 6-inch end for sewing, fasten off. *(5 sc)*

Sew opening closed.

Decs are at top of Beak. Fold Beak in half along decs. Join yellow with **fpsc** (*see Stitch Guide*) around post of first st at right-hand edge, fpsc around post of each rem st across fold. Fasten off. Fold Beak flat, centering post sts on top. With mustard, fpsc around each st on fold at sides of Beak. Fasten off.

Stuff, leaving 1 inch at tip of Beak unstuffed. Sew rnd 1 to Head between rnds 4–14.

## Eye
**Make 2.**

### Background
**Rnd 1:** With yellow, ch 2, 8 sc in 2nd ch from hook. *(8 sc)*

**Rnd 2:** 2 sc in each sc around. *(16 sc)*

**Row 3:** Now working in rows, sc in each of first 4 sc, leaving rem sc unworked, turn. *(4 sc)*

**Row 4:** Ch 1, sc dec in first 2 sc, sc dec in last 2 sc, turn. *(2 sc)*

**Row 5:** Ch 1, sc dec in 2 sc, turn. *(1 sc)*

**Row 6:** Ch 1, sc in sc. Fasten off.

### Iris
With azure, ch 2, 8 sc in 2nd ch from hook, join in first sc. Fasten off. Sew to rnd 1 of Background.

### Pupil
With black, ch 2, 4 sc in 2nd ch from hook, join in first sc. Fasten off.

Sew to center of Iris. Sew Eyes on side of Head ½ inch from Beak.

## Chest
**Row 1:** With white, ch 8, sc in 2nd ch from hook, sc in each rem ch across, turn. *(7 sc)*

**Row 2:** Ch 1, 2 sc in first sc, [sc in each of next 2 sc, 2 sc in next sc] twice, turn. *(10 sc)*

**Row 3:** Ch 1, sc in each sc across, turn.

**Row 4:** Ch 1, 2 sc in first sc, sc in each sc across to last sc, 2 sc in last sc, turn. *(12 sc)*

**Row 5:** Rep row 3.

**Row 6:** Ch 1, 2 sc in first sc, sc in each of next 4 sc, 2 sc in next sc, sc in each of next 5 sc, 2 sc in last sc, turn. *(15 sc)*

**Row 7:** Rep row 3.

**Row 8:** Ch 1, 2 sc in first sc, sc in each of next 6 sc, 2 sc in next sc, sc in each of next 6 sc, 2 sc in last sc, turn. *(18 sc)*

**Row 9:** Rep row 3.

**Row 10:** Ch 1, 2 sc in first sc, sc in each of next 7 sc, 2 sc in next sc, sc in each of next 8 sc, 2 sc in last sc, turn. *(21 sc)*

**Rows 11–17:** Rep row 3.

**Row 18:** Ch 1, sc dec in first 2 sc, sc in each sc across to last 2 sc, sc dec in last 2 sc, turn. *(19 sc)*

**Rows 19–23:** Rep row 18. At end of last row, fasten off. *(9 sc at end of last row)*

Sew to Body with row 1 directly under Beak.

## Wing
**Make 4.**

**Rnd 1:** With black, ch 2, 6 sc in 2nd ch from hook. *(6 sc)*

**Rnd 2:** Ch 1, 2 sc in each sc across, turn. *(12 sc)*

**Rnd 3:** [Sc in next sc, 2 sc in next sc] around. *(18 sc)*

**Rnd 4:** [Sc in each of next 2 sc, 2 sc in next sc] around. *(24 sc)*

**Rnd 5:** [Sc in each of next 3 sc, 2 sc in next sc] around. *(30 sc)*

**Rnd 6:** [Sc in each of next 4 sc, 2 sc in next sc] around. *(36 sc)*

**Rnd 7:** [Sc in each of next 5 sc, 2 sc in next sc] around. *(42 sc)*

**Rnd 8:** [Sc in each of next 6 sc, 2 sc in next sc] around. *(48 sc)*

**Rnd 9:** Sc in each sc around.

**Row 10:** Now working in rows, sc in each of next 10 sc, leaving rem sc unworked, turn. *(10 sc)*

**Row 11:** Ch 1, sc dec in first 2 sc, sc in each rem sc across to last 2 sc, sc dec in last 2 sc, turn. *(8 sc)*

**Rows 12 & 13:** Rep row 11. *(4 sc at end of last row)*

**Row 14:** Ch 1, sc dec in first 2 sc, sc dec in last 2 sc, turn. *(2 sc)*

**Row 15:** Ch 1, sc dec in 2 sc. Fasten off. *(1 sc)*

## Edging

Hold 2 pieces with WS tog; working through both thicknesses, join black with sc, sc in each sc and in end of each row around, working 3 sc in sc of row 15, join in first sc. Fasten off.

Rep with rem 2 pieces. With tip of Wings at back of Body, sew rounded end of Wings on side of Body, 1 inch from edge of Chest.

## Tail Feather
**Make 3.**

**Row 1:** With black, ch 20, sc in 2nd ch from hook, sc in each of next 17 chs, 3 sc in last ch, working in unused lps on opposite side of foundation ch, sc in each of next 18 chs, turn. *(39 sc)*

**Row 2: Ch 3** *(see Pattern Notes)*, dc in each of next 17 sc, 2 dc in each of next 3 sc, dc in each of next 18 sc. Fasten off. *(42 sc)*

Sew ends of 2 Feathers across rnd 35 at back of Body. Sew last Feather centered above first 2.

## Foot
**Make 2.**

**Rnd 1:** With mustard, ch 2, 6 sc in 2nd ch from hook. *(6 sc)*

**Rnd 2:** 2 sc in each sc around. *(12 sc)*

**Rnd 3:** Sc in each sc around.

**Rnds 4–23:** Rep rnd 3.

**Rnd 24:** [Sc in each of next 2 sc, 2 sc in next sc] around. *(16 sc)*

Stuff.

## First Toe
**Rnd 25:** Sc in each of next 3 sc, ch 1, sk next 11 sc, sc in each of next 2 sc. *(5 sc)*

**Rnd 26:** Sc in each of next 3 sc, sc in next ch-1 sp, sc in each of next 2 sc. *(6 sc)*

**Rnds 27–30:** Rep rnd 3.

Stuff.

**Rnd 31:** [Sc dec in next 2 sc] around until opening is closed. Fasten off.

## 2nd Toe
**Rnd 1:** Join mustard with sc in 4th sc on rnd 24, sc in each of next 2 sc, ch 1, sk next 6 sc, sc in each of next 2 sc. *(5 sc)*

**Rnds 2–7:** Rep rnds 26–31 of First Toe.

## 3rd Toe
**Rnd 1:** Join mustard with sc in 7th sc on rnd 24, sc in each of next 5 sc. *(6 sc)*

**Rnds 2–7:** Rep rnds 26–31 of First Toe.

Sew openings between Toes closed. Referring to photo for placement, sew Feet to bottom of Body. ●

# Orson Owl

## Skill Level
 EASY

## Finished Measurement
12 inches tall

## Gauge
4 sc = 1 inch; 4 sc rows = 1 inch

## Pattern Notes
Weave in ends as work progresses.

Work in continuous rounds; do not join or turn unless otherwise stated.

Mark first stitch of round. Move marker up with each round.

Join with slip stitch as indicated unless otherwise stated.

## Materials
- Premier Yarns Deborah Norville Everyday Soft Worsted medium (worsted) weight acrylic yarn (4 oz/203 yds/113g per skein):

  **4 MEDIUM**

    2 skeins each #1002 cream and #1034 terra-cotta

    1 skein #1022 bittersweet

    3 yds #1012 black
- Size G/6/4mm crochet hook or size needed to obtain gauge
- Tapestry needle
- Polyester fiberfill
- Stitch marker
- Small hairbrush

*Need help?*
**StitchGuide.com**
ILLUSTRATED GUIDES
HOW-TO VIDEOS

## Owl

### Head & Body

**Rnd 1:** Starting at top of Head with cream, ch 2, 6 sc in 2nd ch from hook, **do not join, place marker** *(see Pattern Notes)*. *(6 sc)*

**Rnd 2:** 2 sc in each sc around. *(12 sc)*

**Rnd 3:** [Sc in next sc, 2 sc in next st] around. *(18 sc)*

**Rnd 4:** [Sc in each of next 2 sc, 2 sc in next sc] around. *(24 sc)*

**Rnd 5:** [Sc in each of next 3 sc, 2 sc in next sc] around. *(30 sc)*

**Rnd 6:** [Sc in each of next 4 sc, 2 sc in next sc] around. *(36 sc)*

**Rnd 7:** [Sc in each of next 5 sc, 2 sc in next sc] around. *(42 sc)*

**Rnd 8:** Sc in each sc around.

**Rnd 9:** [Sc in each of next 6 sc, 2 sc in next sc] around. *(48 sc)*

**Rnd 10:** Rep rnd 8.

**Rnd 11:** [Sc in each of next 7 sc, 2 sc in next sc] around. *(54 sc)*

**Rnds 12–22:** Rep rnd 8.

**Rnd 23:** [Sc in each of next 8 sc, 2 sc in next sc] around. *(60 sc)*

**Rnd 24:** Rep rnd 8.

**Rnd 25:** [Sc in each of next 5 sc, 2 sc in next sc] around. *(70 sc)*

**Rnd 26:** Rep rnd 8.

**Rnd 27:** [Sc in each of next 6 sc, 2 sc in next sc] around. *(80 sc)*

**Rnd 28:** Rep rnd 8.

Stuff with fiberfill.

**Rnd 29:** [Sc in each of next 7 sc, 2 sc in next sc] around. *(90 sc)*

**Rnds 30–49:** Rep rnd 8.

**Rnd 50:** [Sc in each of next 7 sc, **sc dec** *(see Stitch Guide)* in next 2 sc] around. *(80 sc)*

**Rnd 51:** [Sc in each of next 6 sc, sc dec in next 2 sc] around. *(70 sc)*

**Rnd 52:** [Sc in each of next 5 sc, sc dec in next 2 sc] around. *(60 sc)*

**Rnd 53:** [Sc in each of next 4 sc, sc dec in next 2 sc] around. *(50 sc)*

**Rnd 54:** [Sc in each of next 3 sc, sc dec in next 2 sc] around. *(40 sc)*

**Rnd 55:** [Sc in each of next 2 sc, sc dec in next 2 sc] around. *(30 sc)*

**Rnd 56:** [Sc in next sc, sc dec in next 2 sc] around. *(20 sc)*

Stuff with fiberfill.

**Rnd 57:** [Sc dec in next 2 sc] around. *(10 sc)*

**Rnd 58:** [Sc dec in next 2 sc] 5 times. Leaving 6-inch end for sewing, fasten off. *(5 sc)*

Sew opening closed.

### Pupil
**Make 2.**

With black, ch 2, 4 sc in 2nd ch from hook, **join** *(see Pattern Notes)* in first sc. Fasten off.

### Eye
**Make 2.**

**Rnd 1:** With bittersweet, ch 2, 7 sc in 2nd ch from hook, join in first sc. *(7 sc)*

**Rnd 2:** Ch 1, sc in same sc as beg ch-1, 2 sc in next sc, [sc in next sc, 2 sc in next sc] twice, sc in next sc, join in first sc.

**Rnd 3:** Join black in any sc, sl st in each st around. Fasten off.

Sew Pupils to center of Eyes.

## Fringe

For Fringe, cut 1 strand of terra-cotta 4 inches long. Fold strand in half, insert hook in st, pull folded end through, pull ends through fold, pull ends to tighten knot. Fray ends of yarn and brush to fluff. Work Fringe in each st around each Eye. Referring to photo for placement, sew Eyes to front of Head with Fringe overlapping.

## Beak

**Rnd 1:** With bittersweet, ch 7, join in first ch to form ring, sc in each ch around. *(7 sc)*

**Rnd 2:** Sc in each sc around.

**Rnd 3:** [Sc dec in next 2 sc] 3 times, sc in next sc. *(4 sc)*

**Rnd 4:** [Sc dec in next 2 sc] twice, leaving 6-inch end for sewing, fasten off.

Sew opening closed, stuffing lightly. Sew to Head between Eyes.

## Eyebrows

**Row 1:** With terra-cotta, ch 18, sc in 2nd ch from hook, sc in each of next 7 chs, 3 sc in next ch, sc in each of next 8 chs, turn. *(19 sc)*

**Row 2:** Ch 1, sc in each of first 9 sc, 3 sc in next sc, sc in each of next 9 sc. Fasten off. *(21 sc)*

Referring to photo for placement, sew Eyebrows to Head with point between Eyes.

## Ear
**Make 2.**

**Row 1:** With 2 strands of terra-cotta held tog, ch 7, sc in 2nd ch from hook, sc in each rem ch across, turn. *(6 sc)*

**Row 2:** Ch 1, sc in each sc across, turn.

**Row 3:** Ch 1, sc in each of first 2 sc, sc dec in next 2 sc, sc in each of last 2 sc, turn. *(5 sc)*

**Row 4:** Ch 1, sc in each of first 2 sc, sc dec in next 2 sc, sc in last sc, turn. *(4 sc)*

**Row 5:** Ch 1, sc in first sc, sc dec in next 2 sc, sc in last sc, turn. *(3 sc)*

**Row 6:** Ch 1, sc in first sc, sc dec in next 2 sc. Fasten off. *(2 sc)*

Curving row 1 of Ears around end of Eyebrows, sew to Head.

## Wing
**Make 2.**

**Row 1:** With terra-cotta, ch 16, sc in 2nd ch from hook, sc in each rem ch across, turn. *(15 sc)*

**Row 2:** Ch 1, sc in each sc across, turn.

**Rows 3–12:** Rep row 2.

**Row 13:** Ch 1, sc in each of first 6 sc, sc dec in next 2 sc, sc in each of last 7 sc, turn. *(14 sc)*

**Row 14:** Ch 1, sc in each of first 6 sc, sc dec in next 2 sc, sc in each of last 6 sc, turn. *(13 sc)*

**Row 15:** Ch 1, sc in each of first 5 sc, sc dec in next 2 sc, sc in each of last 6 sc, turn. *(12 sc)*

**Row 16:** Ch 1, sc in each of first 5 sc, sc dec in next 2 sc, sc in each of last 5 sc, turn. *(11 sc)*

**Row 17:** Ch 1, sc in each of first 4 sc, sc dec in next 2 sc, sc in each of last 5 sc, turn. *(10 sc)*

**Row 18:** Ch 1, sc in each of first 4 sc, sc dec in next 2 sc, sc in each of last 4 sc, turn. *(9 sc)*

**Row 19:** Ch 1, sc in each of first 3 sc, sc dec in next 2 sc, sc in each of last 4 sc, turn. *(8 sc)*

**Row 20:** Ch 1, sc in each of first 3 sc, sc dec in next 2 sc, sc in each of last 3 sc, turn. *(7 sc)*

**Row 21:** Ch 1, sc in each of first 2 sc, sc dec in next 2 sc, sc in each of last 3 sc, turn. *(6 sc)*

**Row 22:** Ch 1, sc in each of first 2 sc, sc dec in next 2 sc, sc in each of last 2 sc, turn. *(5 sc)*

**Row 23:** Ch 1, sc in each of first 2 sc, sc dec in next 2 sc, sc in last sc, turn. *(4 sc)*

**Row 24:** Ch 1, sc in first sc, sc dec in next 2 sc, sc in last sc, turn. *(3 sc)*

**Row 25:** Ch 1, sc dec in first 2 sc, sc in last sc, turn. *(2 sc)*

**Row 26:** Ch 1, sc dec in 2 sc. Fasten off. *(1 sc)*

**Row 27:** Join terra-cotta with sc in end of row 1, sc in end of each row around edge to opposite end of row 1, working 3 sc in sc on row 26. Fasten off.

## Fringe

Work Fringe in each sc on row 27 of each Wing same as Fringe for Eyes.

## Foot
**Make 4.**

**Row 1:** With bittersweet, ch 3, sc in 2nd ch from hook, sc in next ch, turn. *(2 sc)*

**Row 2:** Ch 1, sc in each sc across, turn.

**Row 3:** Ch 1, 2 sc in first sc, sc in last sc, turn. *(3 sc)*

**Row 4:** Rep row 2.

**Row 5:** Ch 1, sc in first sc, 2 sc in next sc, sc in last sc, turn. *(4 sc)*

**Row 6:** Rep row 2.

**Row 7:** Ch 1, sc in each of first 2 sc, 2 sc in next sc, sc in last sc, turn. *(5 sc)*

**Rows 8 & 9:** Rep row 2.

**Row 10:** Ch 1, sc in each of first 2 sc, 2 sc in next sc, sc in each of last 2 sc, turn. *(6 sc)*

**Row 11:** Rep row 2.

### First Toe
**Row 12:** Ch 1, sc in each of first 2 sc, leaving rem sts unworked, turn. *(2 sc)*

**Rows 13–15:** Rep row 2.

**Row 16:** Ch 1, sc dec in 2 sc, turn. *(1 sc)*

**Row 17:** Ch 1, sc in sc. Fasten off.

### 2nd Toe
**Row 1:** Join bittersweet with sc in 3rd sc on row 11, sc in next sc, leaving rem sc unworked, turn. *(2 sc)*

**Rows 2–6:** Rep rows 13–17 of First Toe.

### 3rd Toe
**Row 1:** Join bittersweet with sc in 5th sc on row 11, sc in next sc, turn. *(2 sc)*

**Rows 2–6:** Rep rows 13–17 of First Toe.

For each Foot, sew 2 pieces tog. Referring to photo for placement, sew feet to bottom of Body. ●

# Bernard Buzzard

## Skill Level

 ■■□□ EASY

## Finished Measurement

10 inches tall

## Materials

- Premier Yarns Deborah Norville Everyday Soft Worsted medium (worsted) weight acrylic yarn (4 oz/203 yds/113g per skein):
  - 2 skeins #1012 black
  - 1 skein each #1002 cream, #1001 snow white and #1022 bittersweet
  - 3 yds #1023 mist
- Size G/6/4mm crochet hook or size needed to obtain gauge
- Tapestry needle
- Polyester fiberfill
- Stitch marker
- Small hairbrush

## Gauge

4 sc = 1 inch; 4 sc rows = 1 inch

## Pattern Notes

Weave in ends as work progresses.

Work in continuous rounds; do not join or turn unless otherwise stated.

Mark first stitch of round. Move marker up with each round.

Join with slip stitch as indicated unless otherwise stated.

## Buzzard

### Body

**Rnd 1:** With black, ch 2, 6 sc in 2nd ch from hook, **do not join, place marker** (see Pattern Notes). (6 sc)

**Rnd 2:** 2 sc in each sc around. (12 sc)

**Rnd 3:** [Sc in next sc, 2 sc in next st] around. (18 sc)

**Rnd 4:** [Sc in each of next 2 sc, 2 sc in next sc] around. (24 sc)

**Rnd 5:** [Sc in each of next 3 sc, 2 sc in next sc] around. (30 sc)

**Rnd 6:** [Sc in each of next 4 sc, 2 sc in next sc] around. (36 sc)

**Rnd 7:** [Sc in each of next 5 sc, 2 sc in next sc] around. (42 sc)

**Rnd 8:** [Sc in each of next 6 sc, 2 sc in next sc] around. (48 sc)

**Rnd 9:** [Sc in each of next 7 sc, 2 sc in next sc] around. (54 sc)

**Rnd 10:** [Sc in each of next 8 sc, 2 sc in next sc] around. (60 sc)

**Rnd 11:** [Sc in each of next 9 sc, 2 sc in next sc] around. (66 sc)

**Rnd 12:** [Sc in each of next 10 sc, 2 sc in next sc] around. (72 sc)

**Rnd 13:** Sc in each st around.

**Rnds 14–24:** Rep rnd 13.

**Rnd 25:** *Sc in each of next 10 sc, **sc dec** (see Stitch Guide) in next 2 sc, rep from * around. (66 sc)

**Rnd 26:** [Sc in each of next 9 sc, sc dec in next 2 sc] around. (60 sc)

**Rnd 27:** [Sc in each of next 8 sc, sc dec in next 2 sc] around. *(54 sc)*

**Rnd 28:** [Sc in each of next 7 sc, sc dec in next 2 sc] around. *(48 sc)*

**Rnd 29:** [Sc in each of next 6 sc, sc dec in next 2 sc] around. *(42 sc)*

**Rnd 30:** [Sc in each of next 5 sc, sc dec in next 2 sc] around. *(36 sc)*

**Rnd 31:** [Sc in each of next 4 sc, sc dec in next 2 sc] around. *(30 sc)*

**Rnd 32:** [Sc in each of next 3 sc, sc dec in next 2 sc] around. *(24 sc)*

**Rnd 33:** [Sc in each of next 2 sc, sc dec in next 2 sc] around. *(18 sc)*

Stuff with fiberfill.

**Rnd 34:** [Sc in next sc, sc dec in next 2 sc] 6 times. *(12 sc)*

**Rnd 35:** [Sc dec in next 2 sc] 6 times. Leaving 6-inch end for sewing, fasten off. *(6 sc)*

Stuff firmly. Sew opening closed.

## Head
**Rnds 1–4:** With cream, rep rnds 1–4 of Body.

**Rnd 5:** [3 sc in next sc, sc in each of next 5 sc] 4 times. *(32 sc)*

**Rnd 6:** Sc in next sc, [3 sc in next sc, sc in each of next 7 sc] 3 times, 3 sc in next sc, sc in each of next 6 sc. *(40 sc)*

**Rnd 7:** Sc in each sc around.

**Rnds 8 & 9:** Rep rnd 7.

**Rnd 10:** Sc in each of next 2 sc, [sc dec in next 2 sc, sc in each of next 8 sc] 3 times, sc dec in next 2 sc, sc in each of next 6 sc. *(36 sc)*

**Rnds 11–15:** Rep rnd 7. At end of last rnd, leaving 12-inch end for sewing, fasten off.

Stuff.

Referring to photo, sew to rnds 1–12 on upper half of Body.

## Fringe
For Fringe, cut 1 strand of white 4½ inches long. Fold strand in half, insert hook in st, pull folded end through, pull ends through fold, pull ends to tighten knot. Fray ends of yarn and brush to fluff. Work Fringe in rows 12–15 around Head, leaving 2 inches unworked at front.

## Beak
**Rnd 1:** With bittersweet, ch 10, **join** *(see Pattern Notes)* in first ch to form ring, ch 1, sc in each ch around. *(10 sc)*

**Rnd 2:** Sc dec in next 2 sc, sc in each rem sc around. *(9 sc)*

**Rnds 3–7:** Rep rnd 2. At end of last rnd, leaving 6-inch end for sewing, fasten off. *(4 sc at end of last rnd)*

Sew Beak to rnds 3–6 of Head. With tapestry needle and black, embroider **straight stitches** *(see illustration)* at top of Beak for nostrils, and **backstitch** *(see illustration)* mouth lines around sides of Beak.

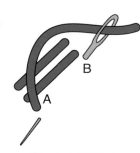

**Straight Stitch**

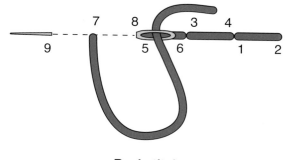

**Backstitch**

## Eye
**Make 2.**

With white, ch 2, 8 sc in 2nd ch from hook, join in first sc. Fasten off.

## Pupil
**Make 2.**

With black, ch 2, 4 sc in 2nd ch from hook, join in first sc. Fasten off.

Sew 1 Pupil to each Eye. Referring to photo, sew Eyes to Head above Beak, 1 inch apart with Pupils in cockeyed position.

## Eyelid
**Make 2.**

**Row 1:** With mist, ch 2, 3 sc in 2nd ch from hook, turn. *(3 sc)*

**Row 2:** Ch 1, 2 sc in first sc, sc in next sc, 2 sc in last sc, turn. *(5 sc)*

**Row 3:** Ch 1, sc in each of first 2 sc, 2 sc in next sc, sc in each of last 2 sc. Fasten off. *(6 sc)*

Sew over top half of each Eye.

## Wing
**Make 2.**

**Row 1:** With black, ch 15, sc in 2nd ch from hook, sc in each rem ch across, turn. *(14 sc)*

**Row 2:** Ch 1, 2 sc in first sc, sc in each rem sc across, turn. *(15 sc)*

**Rows 3–7:** Rep row 2. *(20 sc at end of last row)*

**Row 8:** Ch 1, sc in each sc across, turn.

**Rows 9–15:** Rep row 8.

**Row 16:** Ch 1, sc dec in first 2 sc, sc in each rem sc across, turn. *(19 sts)*

**Rows 17–20:** Rep row 16. *(15 sc at end of last row)*

**Row 21:** Ch 1, sc dec in first 2 sc, sc in each sc across to last 2 sc, sc dec in last 2 sc, turn. *(13 sts)*

**Rows 22–26:** Rep row 21. *(3 sc at end of last row)*

**Row 27:** Ch 1, sc dec in first 2 sc. Leaving rem sc unworked, fasten off.

Sew row 1 of Wings to rows 14–28 of Body, 3 inches apart.

## Leg
**Make 2.**

**Rnd 1:** With black, ch 10, join in first ch to form ring, sc in each ch around. *(10 sc)*

**Rnd 2:** [Sc in each of next 2 sc, 2 sc in next sc] 3 times, sc in next sc. *(13 sc)*

**Rnd 3:** [Sc in each of next 3 sc, 2 sc in next sc] 3 times, sc in next sc. *(16 sc)*

**Rnd 4:** [Sc in each of next 4 sc, 2 sc in next sc] 3 times, sc in next sc. *(19 sc)*

**Rnd 5:** [Sc in each of next 5 sc, 2 sc in next sc] 3 times, sc in next sc. *(22 sc)*

**Rnd 6:** [Sc in each of next 6 sc, 2 sc in next sc] 3 times, sc in next sc. *(25 sc)*

**Rnd 7:** [Sc in each of next 7 sc, 2 sc in next sc] 3 times, sc in next sc. *(28 sc)*

**Rnd 8:** Ch 1, sc in each sc around.

**Rnds 9–13:** Rep rnd 8. At end of last rnd, fasten off.

Stuff. Sew rnd 13 of Legs to rnds 24–32 of bottom of Body.

## Foot
**Make 2.**

**Rnd 1:** With bittersweet, ch 2, 8 sc in 2nd ch from hook. *(8 sc)*

**Rnd 2:** Sc in each sc around.

**Rnds 3–8:** Rep rnd 2.

**Rnd 9:** [Sc in next sc, 2 sc in next sc] 4 times. *(12 sc)*

**Rnd 10:** [Sc in each of next 3 sc, 2 sc in next sc] 3 times. *(15 sc)*

Stuff.

## First Toe
**Rnd 11:** Sc in each of next 5 sc, leave rem sc unworked. *(5 sc)*

**Rnds 12–17:** Rep rnd 2.

Stuff.

**Rnd 18:** [Sc dec in next 2 sc] twice, sc in next sc. Leaving 6-inch end for sewing, fasten off. *(3 sc)*

Sew opening closed.

## 2nd Toe
**Rnd 1:** Join bittersweet with sc in 6th sc on rnd 10, sc in each of next 4 sc, leave rem sc unworked. *(5 sc)*

**Rnds 2–8:** Rep rnds 12–18 of First Toe.

## 3rd Toe
**Rnd 1:** Join bittersweet with sc in 11th sc on rnd 10, sc in each of next 4 sc, leave rem sc unworked. *(5 sc)*

**Rnds 2–8:** Rep rnds 12–18 of First Toe.

Sew center of each Foot to bottom of each Leg.

## Tail
**Row 1:** With black, ch 12, sc in 2nd ch from hook, sc in each rem ch across, turn. *(11 sc)*

**Note:** *Remainder of tail is worked in* **back lps only** *(see Stitch Guide).*

**Row 2:** Ch 1, sc in each of first 5 sc, 3 sc in next sc, sc in each of last 5 sc, turn. *(13 sc)*

**Row 3:** Ch 1, sc in each sc across, turn.

**Row 4:** Ch 1, sc in each of first 6 sc, 3 sc in next sc, sc in each of last 6 sc, turn. *(15 sc)*

**Row 5:** Rep row 3.

**Row 6:** Ch 1, sc in each of first 7 sc, 3 sc in next sc, sc in each of last 7 sc, turn. *(17 sc)*

**Row 7:** Rep row 3.

**Row 8:** Ch 1, sc in each of first 8 sc, 3 sc in next sc, sc in each of last 8 sc, turn. *(19 sc)*

**Row 9:** Rep row 3.

**Row 10:** Ch 1, sc in each of first 9 sc, 3 sc in next sc, sc in each of last 9 sc, turn. *(21 sc)*

**Row 11:** Rep row 3.

**Row 12:** Ch 1, sc in each of first 10 sc, 3 sc in next sc, sc in each of last 10 sc, turn. *(23 sc)*

**Row 13:** Rep row 3.

**Row 14:** Ch 1, sc in each of first 11 sc, 3 sc in next sc, sc in each of last 11 sc, turn. *(25 sc)*

**Row 15:** Rep row 3.

**Row 16:** Ch 1, sc in each of first 12 sc, 3 sc in next sc, sc in each of last 12 sc, turn. *(27 sc)*

**Row 17:** Rep row 3.

**Row 18:** Ch 1, sk first sc, [6 dc in next sc, sk next sc, sc in next sc, sk next sc] 6 times, 6 dc in next sc, sl st in last sc. Fasten off.

Sew row 1 of Tail to rnd 31 of Body. ●

# STITCH GUIDE

*Need help?* ▶ **StitchGuide.com** • ILLUSTRATED GUIDES • HOW-TO VIDEOS

## STITCH ABBREVIATIONS

| | |
|---|---|
| **beg** | begin/begins/beginning |
| **bpdc** | back post double crochet |
| **bpsc** | back post single crochet |
| **bptr** | back post treble crochet |
| **CC** | contrasting color |
| **ch(s)** | chain(s) |
| **ch-** | refers to chain or space previously made (i.e., ch-1 space) |
| **ch sp(s)** | chain space(s) |
| **cl(s)** | cluster(s) |
| **cm** | centimeter(s) |
| **dc** | double crochet (singular/plural) |
| **dc dec** | double crochet 2 or more stitches together, as indicated |
| **dec** | decrease/decreases/decreasing |
| **dtr** | double treble crochet |
| **ext** | extended |
| **fpdc** | front post double crochet |
| **fpsc** | front post single crochet |
| **fptr** | front post treble crochet |
| **g** | gram(s) |
| **hdc** | half double crochet |
| **hdc dec** | half double crochet 2 or more stitches together, as indicated |
| **inc** | increase/increases/increasing |
| **lp(s)** | loop(s) |
| **MC** | main color |
| **mm** | millimeter(s) |
| **oz** | ounce(s) |
| **pc** | popcorn(s) |
| **rem** | remain/remains/remaining |
| **rep(s)** | repeat(s) |
| **rnd(s)** | round(s) |
| **RS** | right side |
| **sc** | single crochet (singular/plural) |
| **sc dec** | single crochet 2 or more stitches together, as indicated |
| **sk** | skip/skipped/skipping |
| **sl st(s)** | slip stitch(es) |
| **sp(s)** | space(s)/spaced |
| **st(s)** | stitch(es) |
| **tog** | together |
| **tr** | treble crochet |
| **trtr** | triple treble |
| **WS** | wrong side |
| **yd(s)** | yard(s) |
| **yo** | yarn over |

### YARN CONVERSION

| OUNCES TO GRAMS | GRAMS TO OUNCES |
|---|---|
| 1 .......... 28.4 | 25 .......... ⅞ |
| 2 .......... 56.7 | 40 .......... 1⅔ |
| 3 .......... 85.0 | 50 .......... 1¾ |
| 4 .......... 113.4 | 100 .......... 3½ |

| UNITED STATES | | UNITED KINGDOM |
|---|---|---|
| sl st (slip stitch) | = | sc (single crochet) |
| sc (single crochet) | = | dc (double crochet) |
| hdc (half double crochet) | = | htr (half treble crochet) |
| dc (double crochet) | = | tr (treble crochet) |
| tr (treble crochet) | = | dtr (double treble crochet) |
| dtr (double treble crochet) | = | ttr (triple treble crochet) |
| skip | = | miss |

**Single crochet decrease (sc dec):** (Insert hook, yo, draw lp through) in each of the sts indicated, yo, draw through all lps on hook.

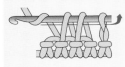

Example of 2-sc dec

**Half double crochet decrease (hdc dec):** (Yo, insert hook, yo, draw lp through) in each of the sts indicated, yo, draw through all lps on hook.

Example of 2-hdc dec

**Reverse single crochet (reverse sc):** Ch 1, sk first st, working from left to right, insert hook in next st from front to back, draw up lp on hook, yo and draw through both lps on hook.

**Chain (ch):** Yo, pull through lp on hook.

**Single crochet (sc):** Insert hook in st, yo, pull through st, yo, pull through both lps on hook.

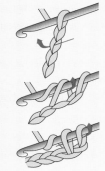

**Double crochet (dc):** Yo, insert hook in st, yo, pull through st, [yo, pull through 2 lps] twice.

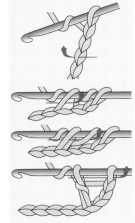

**Double crochet decrease (dc dec):** (Yo, insert hook, yo, draw lp through, yo, draw through 2 lps on hook) in each of the sts indicated, yo, draw through all lps on hook.

Example of 2-dc dec

**Front loop (front lp) Back loop (back lp)**

Front Loop   Back Loop

**Front post stitch (fp): Back post stitch (bp):** When working post st, insert hook from right to left around post of st on previous row.

Back   Front

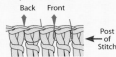

Post of Stitch

**Half double crochet (hdc):** Yo, insert hook in st, yo, pull through st, yo, pull through all 3 lps on hook.

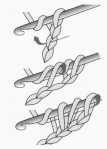

**Double treble crochet (dtr):** Yo 3 times, insert hook in st, yo, pull through st, [yo, pull through 2 lps] 4 times.

**Treble crochet decrease (tr dec):** Holding back last lp of each st, tr in each of the sts indicated, yo, pull through all lps on hook.

Example of 2-tr dec

**Slip stitch (sl st):** Insert hook in st, pull through both lps on hook.

**Chain color change (ch color change)** Yo with new color, draw through last lp on hook.

**Double crochet color change (dc color change)** Drop first color, yo with new color, draw through last 2 lps of st.

**Treble crochet (tr):** Yo twice, insert hook in st, yo, pull through st, [yo, pull through 2 lps] 3 times.

# Metric Conversion Charts

## METRIC CONVERSIONS

| | | | | |
|---|---|---|---|---|
| yards | x | .9144 | = | metres (m) |
| yards | x | 91.44 | = | centimetres (cm) |
| inches | x | 2.54 | = | centimetres (cm) |
| inches | x | 25.40 | = | millimetres (mm) |
| inches | x | .0254 | = | metres (m) |

| | | | | |
|---|---|---|---|---|
| centimetres | x | .3937 | = | inches |
| metres | x | 1.0936 | = | yards |

## INCHES INTO MILLIMETRES & CENTIMETRES (Rounded off slightly)

| inches | mm | cm | inches | cm | inches | cm | inches | cm |
|---|---|---|---|---|---|---|---|---|
| 1/8 | 3 | 0.3 | 5 | 12.5 | 21 | 53.5 | 38 | 96.5 |
| 1/4 | 6 | 0.6 | 5 1/2 | 14 | 22 | 56 | 39 | 99 |
| 3/8 | 10 | 1 | 6 | 15 | 23 | 58.5 | 40 | 101.5 |
| 1/2 | 13 | 1.3 | 7 | 18 | 24 | 61 | 41 | 104 |
| 5/8 | 15 | 1.5 | 8 | 20.5 | 25 | 63.5 | 42 | 106.5 |
| 3/4 | 20 | 2 | 9 | 23 | 26 | 66 | 43 | 109 |
| 7/8 | 22 | 2.2 | 10 | 25.5 | 27 | 68.5 | 44 | 112 |
| 1 | 25 | 2.5 | 11 | 28 | 28 | 71 | 45 | 114.5 |
| 1 1/4 | 32 | 3.2 | 12 | 30.5 | 29 | 73.5 | 46 | 117 |
| 1 1/2 | 38 | 3.8 | 13 | 33 | 30 | 76 | 47 | 119.5 |
| 1 3/4 | 45 | 4.5 | 14 | 35.5 | 31 | 79 | 48 | 122 |
| 2 | 50 | 5 | 15 | 38 | 32 | 81.5 | 49 | 124.5 |
| 2 1/2 | 65 | 6.5 | 16 | 40.5 | 33 | 84 | 50 | 127 |
| 3 | 75 | 7.5 | 17 | 43 | 34 | 86.5 | | |
| 3 1/2 | 90 | 9 | 18 | 46 | 35 | 89 | | |
| 4 | 100 | 10 | 19 | 48.5 | 36 | 91.5 | | |
| 4 1/2 | 115 | 11.5 | 20 | 51 | 37 | 94 | | |

## KNITTING NEEDLES CONVERSION CHART

| Canada/U.S. | 0 | 1 | 2 | 3 | 4 | 5 | 6 | 7 | 8 | 9 | 10 | 10½ | 11 | 13 | 15 |
|---|---|---|---|---|---|---|---|---|---|---|---|---|---|---|---|
| Metric (mm) | 2 | 2¼ | 2¾ | 3¼ | 3½ | 3¾ | 4 | 4½ | 5 | 5½ | 6 | 6½ | 8 | 9 | 10 |

## CROCHET HOOKS CONVERSION CHART

| Canada/U.S. | 1/B | 2/C | 3/D | 4/E | 5/F | 6/G | 8/H | 9/I | 10/J | 10½/K | N |
|---|---|---|---|---|---|---|---|---|---|---|---|
| Metric (mm) | 2.25 | 2.75 | 3.25 | 3.5 | 3.75 | 4.25 | 5 | 5.5 | 6 | 6.5 | 9.0 |

*Gooney Birds* is published by Annie's, 306 East Parr Road, Berne, IN 46711. Printed in USA. Copyright © 2015 Annie's. All rights reserved. This publication may not be reproduced in part or in whole without written permission from the publisher.

**RETAIL STORES:** If you would like to carry this publication or any other Annie's publication, visit AnniesWSL.com.

Every effort has been made to ensure that the instructions in this publication are complete and accurate. We cannot, however, take responsibility for human error, typographical mistakes or variations in individual work. Please visit AnniesCustomerService.com to check for pattern updates.

ISBN: 978-1-57367-710-3

1 2 3 4 5 6 7 8 9